For my twin grandsons,
John and Michael, who live their
lives with steadfast love.

–C.C.M.

Go and learn what this means, "I desire mercy, and not sacrifice."
Matthew 9:13

In accordance with CIC 827, permission to publish has been granted on October 26, 2021, by the Most Reverend Mark S. Rivituso, Auxiliary Bishop, Archdiocese of St. Louis. Permission to publish is an indication that nothing contrary to Church teaching is contained in this particular work. It does not imply any endorsement of the opinions expressed in the publication, or a general endorsement of any author; nor is any liability assumed by this permission.

Published by Ascension Publishing Group, LLC.

Ascension
PO Box 1990
West Chester, PA 19380

1-800-376-0520
ascensionpress.com

Cover design: Rosemary Strohm

Printed in the United States of America
21 22 23 24 25 5 4 3 2 1

ISBN 978-1-950784-64-6

Louie's Lent

Written by CLAUDIA CANGILLA McADAM
Illustrated by MICHAEL ROGERS

ASCENSION
Kids

West Chester, Pennsylvania

Excitement buzzed through the classroom.
It was Ash Wednesday, and all the kids knew
what they wanted to do for Lent.

2

Everyone, that is, except Louie.

3

"How many days did Jesus spend in the desert?" Sister Mary Lawrence asked.

"Forty!" the kids shouted.

Sister laid her hand over her heart. "Right. Lent is a time for us to change who we are on the inside. We want to become better at following Christ in the way he wants us to live. We imitate Jesus when we pray and fast, like he did."

Beth put up her arm. "I'm giving up sweets," she said.

Miguel raised his hand. "I won't be playing video games."

Sister smiled. "And we can give to those in need. We can even try to break a bad habit."

"Like coming to school late every day," one boy said, as he elbowed J.P.

Ellie stood. "I am going to walk to school on Fridays, instead of getting a ride with my dad."

Louie didn't know what he could do for Lent. He wasn't allowed to eat sweets. His family couldn't afford video games, and he walked to school every day.

In the cafeteria at noon, Beth finished her egg sandwich and apple. Her lips curved in an upside-down smile. There was no cookie in her lunch.

8

Louie only had cheese and crackers, carrot sticks, and a bag of sunflower seeds.

"Here," he said, offering the seeds to Beth.

"Have some of these."

"What are you giving up for Lent?" she asked him.

He shrugged. He couldn't think of anything.

On Friday, Louie woke early so he could walk three blocks in the opposite direction of school. He rang Ellie's doorbell. Her eyebrows shot up when she saw him.

"I thought you might like some company on your way to school," he said.

She snaked her arms into her backpack straps. "What are you doing for Lent?" she asked him.

Louie shrugged. He still hadn't thought of anything.

On the way to school, Louie stopped to make sure J.P. was awake, so he would be on time for class. J.P. opened the door, yawning. "I fell back asleep when Mom left for work," he said to Louie. "Good thing you came by. What bad habit are you trying to break?"

Louie shrugged. He didn't have any bad habits.

On Saturday, Louie saw Miguel at the park. Miguel sat slouched on a bench, his hands in his pockets. "I'm bored since I can't play video games," he said.

"Want to play soccer?" Louie asked.

On the field, preschoolers ran and kicked their soccer balls. "Can we help put the kids through their drills?" Louie asked the coach.

After an hour of running, Miguel high-fived Louie, a big smile on his face.

"What are you giving up for Lent?" Miguel asked as they strolled home.

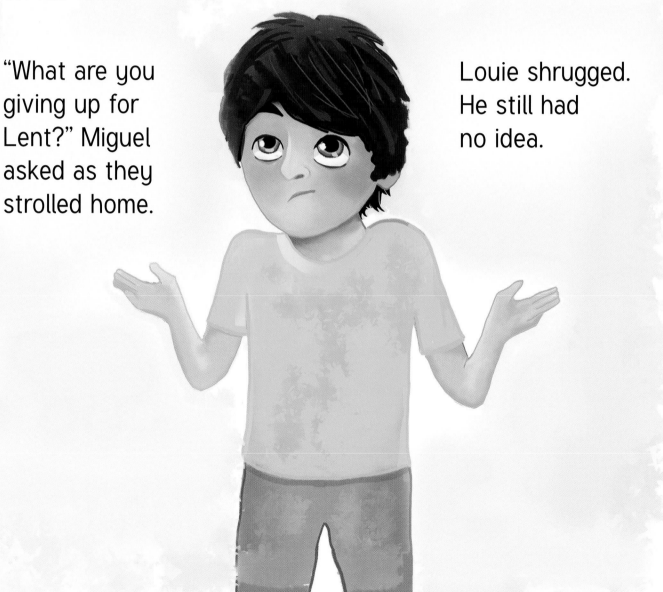

Louie shrugged. He still had no idea.

The forty days of Lent rolled by. Each day, Louie shared his sunflower seeds with Beth.

He walked to school on Fridays with Ellie.

Every morning he knocked on J.P.'s door
to make sure he was awake.

And he met Miguel at the park each Saturday to help with the soccer team.

On Holy Thursday, Sister Mary Lawrence asked the class, "How did your Lent go?"

"Great!" Beth said. "I've missed eating sweets,

but that reminds me of Jesus' suffering."

"When I walk to school," Ellie added, "I see the beauty of God's creation and say a prayer of thanksgiving for it."

"I learned that being with people is more important than playing video games," Miguel told the class.

"I realize that Jesus wants us to do our best at everything," J.P. said, "including getting to school on time."

Louie looked down at his desk.

"Giving up things and changing bad habits are good to do for Lent," Sister Mary Lawrence said, "but there's more to it than that." She pointed to the crucifix.

"Jesus gave his life for us. He wants us to die to our sins and become more like him." She stopped at Louie's desk, and he looked up at her.

"Doing things for other people is like doing them for the Lord."

All the kids looked at each other and then at Louie.

Beth grinned at him. Miguel let out a whistle. Ellie punched her arms into the air. J.P. drummed out a beat on his desk.

Applause thundered across the classroom.

Color crept up
Louie's face as
he smiled and
shrugged.

It had been a good Lent
for him, too.